american
MUSIC MILESTONES

AMERICAN
Latin Music

RUMBA RHYTHMS, BOSSA NOVA, AND THE SALSA SOUND

MATT *DOEDEN*

TFCB

TWENTY-FIRST CENTURY BOOKS
MINNEAPOLIS

NOTE TO READERS: some songs and music videos by artists discussed in this book contain language and images that readers may consider offensive.

Twenty-First Century Books
A division of Lerner Publishing Group, Inc.
241 First Avenue North
Minneapolis, MN 55401 U.S.A.

Website address: www.lernerbooks.com

Library of Congress Cataloging-in-Publication Data

Doeden, Matt.
    American Latin music : rumba rhythms, bossa nova, and the salsa
sound / by Matt Doeden.
        p.   cm. — (American music milestones)
    Includes bibliographical references and index.
    ISBN 978–0–7613–4505–3 (lib. bdg. : alk. paper)
    1. Popular music—United States—Latin American influences.
2. Dance music—Latin America—History and criticism. 3. Music—
Latin America—History and criticism. 4. Musicians—Latin America.
5. Salsa (Music)—History and criticism. I. Title.
ML3477.D64 2013
781.64089'68073—dc23   2012002074

Manufactured in the United States of America
1 – CG – 7/15/12

CONTENTS

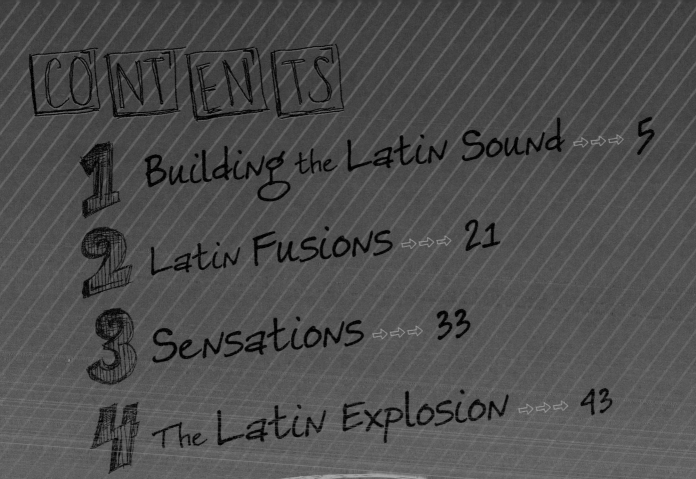

chapter 1

BUILDING THE Latin Sound

Pitbull LEFT, Rodrigo y Gabriela RIGHT, and Shakira FAR RIGHT are some of the biggest names in modern Latin music.

PITBULL'S GRAVELLY VOICE, SHAKIRA'S SULTRY SINGING, AND THE TWIN GUITAR GROOVES OF RODRIGO Y GABRIELA ARE JUST A FEW OF THE SOUNDS OF MODERN LATIN MUSIC.

Latin music has been a part of the United States music scene for more than a century. The Latin world includes the Spanish speaking nations of Central America and the Caribbean as well as the Spanish- and Portuguese-speaking nations of South America. Latin music is a rich blend of cultures.

Spanish, Portuguese, and African sounds form the core of Latin music. Latin music also draws from other European music traditions and from Native American peoples.

Although Spanish is the most common language in Latin music, Portuguese-language speakers have played a major role in the music's history. Latin music also has an undeniable connection to dancing. Fast or slow, there's just something about Latin rhythms that inspires people to get up and move.

Modern Latin music includes a wide range of styles. Each of these styles traces back to a different region or time period. Over time, these styles all moved to the United States. Musicians in the United States have changed and combined different Latin styles to create unique new sounds. Latin music has influenced and been influenced by almost every major form of music in the United States.

SON-RISE

No Latin American country has had a bigger influence on music in the United States than the island of Cuba. Beginning in the 1500s, European settlers brought peoples from western Africa to work as slaves in Cuba. Slavery ended on the island in the 1880s, but many descendants of slaves remained in Cuba. Their African heritage remains a major part of Cuba's culture. Cuban music has a distinct African flavor, with strong rhythms and powerful beats. And because Cuba was settled mainly by the Spanish, Cuban music is usually sung in Spanish.

Son is the ultimate fusion of Spanish and African sounds. This style of music grew out of Cuban folk songs and thrived on the island. Son has a distinct Spanish flavor. Many son songs feature the Spanish guitar. But its distinct African beat makes the son uniquely Cuban.

The son style exploded in 1868. That year, Cubans won independence from Spain, which had controlled the island since the 1500s. After the war, victorious Cuban soldiers streamed into the capital city of Havana. Many of them brought along musical instruments such as guitars, maracas, and bongo drums. Others added the thump of a simple homemade bass

(often just an empty jug) to the mix. Together they had all the elements of the modern son sound.

The son sound took over Cuba. People usually played the music in a group of six called a *sexteto*. The sexteto featured two vocalists. One was a high-voiced tenor who played claves. The other was a low-voiced baritone who played maracas. They were backed by a bass, a bongo drum, a *tres* (a six-stringed guitarlike instrument), and a guiro (a hollowed-out gourd with ridges against which the player drags a stick).

Local musicians in modern-day Cuba keep the son style alive.

A LOOK AT LATIN INSTRUMENTS

Latin music includes a wide variety of instruments. Here's a quick look at some of the instruments that aren't well known to U.S. audiences.

bajo sexto: a Mexican bass guitar that features six pairs of strings, a total of twelve strings

bandoneón: an accordion-like instrument played by pumping its midsection while pressing the buttons on its handles

bongo drums: a pair of open-bottomed drums. Bongos are connected to each other at the side. The larger drum is called the *hembra* (female). The smaller drum is the *macho* (male).

claves: a pair of short, thick sticks. Claves make a sharp clicking sound when struck together.

conga drum: a tall, single-headed drum from Cuba. The conga drum is also called the tumbadora.

guiro: a gourd-shaped percussion instrument. A player rubs a stick along the ridges of a guiro to make a rattling sound.

maracas: gourd-shaped instruments filled with beans or seeds. Maracas are usually played in pairs. A player shakes them to make a rattling sound.

tamborim: a small drum with a closed bottom side. A player strikes a tamborim with a pair of drumsticks to create a high, sharp sound.

tres: a guitar-like instrument from Cuba. The tres includes three pairs of two strings.

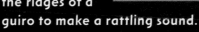

CUBAN SOUNDS HEAD NORTH

Son may have been king in Cuba, but another Cuban sound was first to reach the United States. The gentle bolero style was created by José "Pepe" Sánchez in the late 1800s. Bolero songs centered on storytelling. Love stories were particularly common.

Pepe Sánchez had little formal music training. He composed bolero songs in his head without ever writing them down. For this reason, much of his original bolero music is lost. But Sánchez's fellow musicians were moved by his powerful songs. They wrote down some of the music, and the modern Cuban bolero tradition springs from these musical treasures.

By the start of the twentieth century, the bolero style had spread throughout Cuba. Soon it could be heard in Mexico, Central America, and the United States. Bolero inspired similar styles, including the slow, beautiful bolero mamba; the stirring bolero-son; and the bolero-cha (known for its cha-cha-cha rhythm).

One of the biggest stateside successes was Cuba's Trío Matamoros. Guitarist Miguel Matamoros, guitarist and vocalist Rafeal Cueto, and maraca player Siro Rodríguez made up the group. Miguel Matamoros

Cuba's Trío Matamoros brought son music to the United States in the 1930s.

One of the trademark sounds of Latin music is syncopation. Syncopation is the stressing of a beat that is not normally stressed, or the skipping of a strong beat. Syncopation interrupts the smooth flow of the rhythm in a piece of music. The changeable rhythms of Latin music are part of its lively, danceable appeal and an element of any good Latin dance song. Forms of music such as jazz also use syncopation.

was a brilliant songwriter. Many of the trio's hits of the 1920s and the 1930s blended son and bolero. These hits include "Son de la Loma" ("They Come from the Hill"), "El Que Siembra Su Maíz" ("He Who Sows His Corn"), and "Lágrimas Negras" ("Black Tears"). The bolero-son style captured the attention of the music world. Trío Matamoros toured in Latin America, the United States, and Europe. They often performed at clubs in New York City in the 1930s and the 1940s. Their success helped pave the way for other son artists in the United States.

CUBA CONTINUES
TO SHINE

Rita Montaner was born in Cuba in 1900. She was a noted pianist by the time she was fifteen. By the early 1920s, she was well known in Cuba and across much of Latin America as a pianist and a vocalist. Montaner began recording songs for the U.S. company Columbia

Rita Montaner, pictured here in the 1940s, sang memorable crossover songs such as "El Manicero" ("The Peanut Vendor," 1928).

Records in 1927 and quickly gained stardom in the United States. Her performance of the song "El Manicero" ("The Peanut Vendor," 1928) was a big hit in Europe and in North America. Although acting became the focus of her career later in life, she is still remembered as one of the great Cuban musicians of her time.

While Rita Montaner was growing up, the upbeat sounds of the rumba were echoing in the streets of Cuba. The rumba was pure dance music dominated by percussion instruments. Rumba singers called out to listeners and encouraged them to sing back. Early rumba instruments were often simple household items used as drums. Later, the use of thundering conga drums became the standard. Despite the rumba's popularity, many felt that the movements of rumba dancers were lewd and inappropriate. It wasn't until the 1920s and the 1930s that rumba was accepted in the Cuban mainstream. The rumba gained widespread popularity in the United States several decades after the music's breakthrough in Cuba.

CARLOS GARDEL AND THE NEW TANGO

Carlos Gardel of Buenos Aires, Argentina, was a classically trained vocalist. But he had little interest in classical music. Instead, Gardel was captivated by a style of music straight out of the lower class of Latin America—the tango.

The roots of Latin and jazz are the same. New Orleans at the turn of the century was a very Caribbean city....

Many of the musicians that came back and forth between Cuba and New Orleans...

brought with them some of the rhythms that infected and inflected a lot of what we call jazz.

—Arturo O'Farrill, jazz pianist, 2009

LATIN MUSIC and AMERICAN JAZZ

While people in the United States were discovering the tango, Cuban sounds were also beginning to impact the U.S. music scene. Political conflicts in Cuba and nearby Haiti had driven thousands of people to the southern United States. Many of them entered through the port city of New Orleans, Louisiana.

New Orleans was rich with diversity. It saw immigrants and travelers from around the world. By the early 1900s, it was a true cultural melting pot. Musical styles mingled and crossed over within the city. Musicians in the African American communities of New Orleans drew on global influences while creating the sound known as jazz. Jazz is a rhythmic and often danceable style of music. Jazz songs are marked by musicians' use of improvisation (making decisions in the moment). According to jazz legend Jelly Roll Morton (Ferdinand LaMothe) (RIGHT), "If you can't manage to put tinges of Spanish [Latin music] in your tunes, you will never be able to get the right seasoning, I call it, for jazz."

Tango music developed in poor areas on the edge of Buenos Aires. European immigrants and natives of Argentina added elements to the music throughout the 1800s. The tango sound is a slow, sorrowful mix of brass and string instruments. The music had an unsavory reputation and links to gangster life. It was also linked to the sultry Latin couple's dance of the same name. At the time, tango music was almost entirely instrumental. But Gardel felt that the rhythms of the tango could speak to people the way they spoke to him. He began penning lyrics to go with the music.

In 1917 Gardel unveiled the vocally driven style called *tango canción* (song). He performed his new songs at a concert in Buenos Aires. Music fans loved Gardel's deep voice, smooth-flowing lyrics, and movie-star good looks. He wrote many hit songs, including "Mi Buenos Aires Querido" ("My Beloved Buenos Aires," 1934) and "El Día Que Me Quieras" ("The Day That You Love Me," 1935). However, his version of "Mi Noche Triste" ("My Sorrowful Night," 1917) was the best known of his many hits. Soon others were imitating his style.

With his unique tango canción sound, Gardel was one of the first artists to make Latin music that sold well in the United States. He took a sound that had lived in the darkest corners of Argentinian society

Carlos Gardel, pictured here in 1935, added lyrics to tango music and gained international fame.

and transformed it into something played on a worldwide stage. The tango sound became one of the most widely heard styles of Latin music in the United States. Within a few years, it could be heard in clubs and bars across North America and Europe. Gardel's songs helped to open doors not only for other tango artists but also for entirely different Latin styles.

THE TANGO EVOLVES

Carlos Gardel died in 1935. That year also marked the unofficial beginning of the Golden Age of Tango. Around this time, many people in the United States were dancing to styles of jazz such as big band and swing music. New twists on the tango grew alongside these dance movements.

Traditional tango music uses two violins, a piano, a double bass, and two *bandoneóns* (an instrument related to the accordion). While some artists held true to this form, other artists took the sound to new places. Some even played tango music with full orchestras. Argentinean artists such as Osvaldo Pugliese and Elvino Vardaro became the tango stars of the 1930s. Aníbal Troilo was the biggest name in tango in the 1940s. In spite of the success of these artists, the popularity of the tango began to fade in the 1950s. By that time, new Latin sounds had replaced it in the American music scene.

OUT OF BRAZIL

The tango wasn't the only Latin sound to emerge from South America. The Portuguese-speaking nation of Brazil has also given much to Latin music. The samba emerged in the Brazilian city of Rio de Janeiro. The samba is both a percussion-driven style of music and a dance. Samba musicians play guitars and a wide range of percussion instruments, including the *tamborim*, a small, two-sided drum.

Samba music fuses together many African sounds. It started as a form of folk music among Brazil's freed black slaves. In the 1800s, samba beats were the sound track to the circle dances of African peoples in Brazil. Musicians struck *bombos* (large bass drums) and shook rattles to get dancers moving. The samba evolved into a full-fledged party sound. The first recording of samba music was "Pelo Telefone"

A young New Hampshire couple performs the tango in the 1920s. By this time, the tango had reached the United States. It was a hit among fans of jazz music.

Carmen Miranda strikes a pose in 1947. Known as the Brazilian Bombshell, Miranda enjoyed success in both music and film.

("By Telephone") by Banda Odeon in 1917. Soon the sound took over the Brazilian music scene.

Not everyone embraced samba. At the time, the Brazilian government was controlled mainly by people of European descent. Some members of the government felt threatened by the music of lower-class blacks who had been slaves only a few decades earlier. Until the 1920s, the Brazilian government tried to suppress the sound. By the 1930s, the samba movement had outgrown any government repression. People in the middle and upper classes began to embrace samba music. It became a symbol of national pride. With its lively rhythms, samba was a perfect fit for Rio's famous pre-Easter Carnival celebration, as well as at sporting events.

CARMEN

Carmen Miranda helped bring the samba sound to the United States. She began recording samba music in 1929 and quickly became a star in Brazil. Her talent and good looks caught the attention of U.S. audiences as well. In 1939 Miranda came to the United States to sing and act. Her visit was part of the Good Neighbor Policy. U.S. president Franklin Delano Roosevelt designed this policy to promote good relations between the United States and Latin America. Miranda was every bit as popular in the United States. Because of her striking looks, fans called her the Brazilian Bombshell. She was one of the biggest female movie stars of the 1940s.

Some fans back in Brazil accused her of leaving her roots behind. So Miranda wrote the song "Disseram Que Voltei Americanisada" ("They Say That I Returned Americanized," 1940). It declared her devotion to Brazilian culture. Miranda died in 1955 after suffering a heart attack on live television on *The Jimmy Durante Show*. Her fans in Brazil and around the world were shocked. Half a million people turned out in Rio to pay their respects as her body was carried to its resting place.

THE CUBAN INVASION

By the early 1950s, another Cuban sound had entered the United States. The strong beat and free-flowing dance style of the mambo took off in New York City. The mambo had evolved from Cuban dance music. It was perfected in Mexico by Cuba-born bandleader Pérez Prado. Prado was known as the King of the Mambo.

Cuban and Mexican immigrants brought the mambo with them to New York. New Yorkers quickly embraced the infectious sound as their own. Mambo clubs opened all over the city. Meanwhile, Pérez Prado completed a successful tour of the United States in 1951.

Record companies were quick to take advantage of the trend, signing mambo artists and releasing albums.

Pérez Prado, the King of the Mambo, directs his bandmates in 1955.

BENY MORÉ

Beny Moré (BELOW) is a hero of Cuban music. Moré was born Bartolomé Maximiliano Moré Gutiérrez in central Cuba in 1919. From the start, he had a pure tenor voice and a magnetic stage presence. In 1945 he got his big break. Trío Matamoros needed a fill-in vocalist. Moré fit the bill so well that he went on to record with the group.

Later, Moré joined up with Cuban bandleader Pérez Prado. Together they explored the mambo rhythm. Prado's flair for musical arrangement perfectly suited Moré's smooth vocals. The two musicians played a huge role in launching the mambo craze of the 1950s. In 1951 Moré formed his own eighteen-piece band, La Banda Gigante. He and the band recorded many hits, including "Bonito y Sabroso" ("Beautiful and Tasty," 1952).

It was a cross-cultural fad. People of all backgrounds took to the upbeat music and the expressive dance that went along with it. Top dancers and artists such as Frank "Killer Joe" Piro, Pedro "Cuban Pete" Aguilar, and the Mambo Aces gained stardom almost overnight.

Unlike many Latin music fads before it, the mambo wasn't limited to New York or New Orleans. It became popular across the country. The mambo boom was set off by the hugely popular television comedy I Love Lucy. One of the show's stars, Desi Arnaz, was a gifted mambo singer. His song "El Cumbanchero" ("The Brave Combo," 1949) remains one of the most widely known mambos in the world.

A political revolution in the late 1950s cut off Cubans in the United States from their homeland. This left musicians in the United States to develop their own sounds. Musicians such as Johnny Pacheco of the Dominican Republic and Puerto Rican New Yorker Ray Barretto combined classic Latin sounds with American influences, including R & B (rhythm and blues) and rock. The style of music they created was based loosely on son. At first this emerging new style didn't have a name. Later on, it would become known as salsa.

Salsa music was the first true blend of Latin music and American pop. This fusion gave salsa a more lasting appeal among listeners in the United States. Many previous Latin sounds had largely been fads. Salsa was here to stay.

The dance instructor Killer Joe Piro LEFT and the singer Desi Arnaz RIGHT both took part in the mambo boom of the 1950s.

João Gilberto LEFT, Astrud Gilberto BOTTOM LEFT, and Stan Getz BOTTOM RIGHT joined together to record "The Girl from Ipanema" (1964). The song gave listeners in the United States a taste of bossa nova music. Bossa nova songs were stripped down but smooth, usually featuring a single guitar and vocals.

BOSSA NOVA CROSSES OVER

By the late 1950s, a new sound had grown out of Brazil's samba. The bossa nova (new trend) was a cooler, more laid-back version of samba music. It featured more complex harmonies and melodies and fewer percussion sounds. In its purest form, bossa nova featured nothing more than a guitar (played without a pick) and a vocalist. It was designed to be ultrasmooth. Brazilian audiences ate it up. Many credit João Gilberto of Brazil with creating the guitar sound of the bossa nova. Gilberto's 1958 version of the song "Chega de Saudade" ("No More Blues") was the first bossa nova song that many local Brazilians heard.

In 1964 many U.S. residents discovered the bossa nova style. That year, songwriter Norman Gimbel took a Portuguese bossa nova song titled "Garota de Ipanema" and translated it to English. It became "The Girl from Ipanema." João Gilberto, Brazilian singer Astrud Gilberto, and U.S. saxophone player Stan Getz recorded Gimbel's version. Music fans loved the casual tone of the song. "The Girl from Ipanema" reached No. 5 on the U.S. charts. Bossa nova briefly exploded in popularity worldwide. Around the same time, American sounds began to overshadow traditional styles in Latin America. ★

MUST DOWNLOAD Playlist

TRÍO MATAMOROS
"El Que Siembra Su Maíz"
("He Who Sows His Corn,"
1920s)

RITA MONTANER
"El Manicero"
("The Peanut Vendor," 1928)

CARMEN MIRANDA
"Disseram Que Voltei
Americanisada"
("They Say That I Returned
Americanized," 1940),
"I, Yi, Yi, Yi, Yi
(I Like You Very Much)" (1941)

ANÍBAL TROILO
"Barrio de Tango"
("Neighborhood of Tango," 1942)

DESI ARNAZ
"El Cumbanchero"
("The Brave Combo," 1949)

BENY MORÉ
"Conocí La Paz"
("I Found Peace," 1950s),
"Bonito y Sabroso"
("Beautiful and Tasty," 1952)

PÉREZ PRADO
"Cereza Rosa"
("Cherry Pink," 1955)

**STAN GETZ, ASTRUD
GILBERTO, AND JOÃO
GILBERTO**
"The Girl from Ipanema"
(1964)

2 LATIN Fusions

California teenager Ritchie Valens became the first Mexican American rock star with his 1958 hit "La Bamba."

IN THE 1950S, LATIN MUSIC WAS MINGLING WITH POP, JAZZ, AND DANCE MUSIC IN THE UNITED STATES.

One of the most dramatic fusions was the addition of Latin beats to a hot new American trend—rock 'n' roll.

Perhaps no one is more responsible for marrying these two sounds than Mexican American musician Richard Valenzuela. Valenzuela was just a teenager when he was discovered by the owner of a small California record label in the 1950s. The label encouraged Valenzuela to shorten his last name so that it sounded less Mexican. At the time, many white record buyers would have been less likely to check out the music of a nonwhite artist. The rocker Ritchie Valens was born.

Valens was a brilliant guitarist and songwriter. His early work was straight-up rock with little or no Latin influence. Yet his real legacy is his cover of "La Bamba." Valens was fascinated by the Mexican folk song, even though he himself knew only English. His bandmates convinced him to give the song rock 'n' roll flair. In October 1958, he released his rock version of the song. It all but single-handedly started the Latin rock movement. "La Bamba" was a smash. It reached No. 22 on the U.S. pop chart even though it was sung in Spanish.

Valens never got a chance to follow up "La Bamba" with more Latin-themed rock. He was killed in a plane crash in 1959 along with fellow musicians Buddy Holly and J. P. "Big Bopper" Richardson.

LATIN GUITAR LEGEND

Luckily for fans of Latin rock, other artists were there to take his place. Perhaps the greatest Latin rock star of all time is guitarist Carlos Santana. Santana was born in Mexico. In the 1960s, he moved to San Francisco, California. At that time, San Francisco was home to bold rock acts such as Janis Joplin and the Grateful Dead. Santana, a wizard with the guitar, fit right in.

In 1969 Santana and his band (also called Santana) hit the big time after a performance at the famous Woodstock Music and Art Fair in New York. Curious rock fans made the 1970 album **Abraxas** a No. 1 hit. Songs such as "Black Magic Woman" became rock radio staples.

Santana (the band) blended the salsa sound with jazz, blues, and rock. Its music featured Carlos's

Carlos Santana rocks out at the 1969 Woodstock festival in New York State.

bluesy guitar backed by Latin and African beats. Santana songs often included traditional Latin instruments such as conga drums too. Across the decades, Carlos Santana's sound has changed and evolved. But he has always held to his Latin roots.

NUEVA
CANCIÓN

While Latin styles were coming and going in the United States, much of Latin America was experiencing tremendous social changes. In the late 1960s and the early 1970s, struggles for power were taking place within Portugal, Spain, Chile, Argentina, Panama, Puerto Rico, and other nations. These conflicts deeply affected Latin artists.

During this time, a new form of folk music gained popularity among listeners. The *nueva canción* (new song) movement addressed the political struggles of the time. It started in Chile and quickly spread across Latin America and to Europe. Artists such as Chile's Violeta Parra set the tone by playing stripped-down music with traditional instruments. These artists spoke out against war and government corruption. They called for peace and human rights.

Chile's Violeta Parra SEATED inspired the musicians of the nueva canción movement with her tradition-minded folk songs.

BOOGALOO

In the 1960s, many African Americans and Latinos lived in New York City's poorer neighborhoods. Kids from these two different backgrounds introduced each other to new styles of music. Soon the R & B styles popular with many African Americans began to mix with son and mambo styles popular with Latinos. This combination gave rise to a new sound: boogaloo. In 1966 the boogaloo sound hit the big time with "Bang Bang" by New York's Joe Cuba Sextet (LEFT). The catchy boogaloo tune sold more than one million copies.

Cuba's **Silvio Rodríguez** (ABOVE) is perhaps the best-known nueva canción artist in the United States. His landmark 1975 album *Días y Flores (Days and Flowers)* earned him comparisons to U.S. folksinger Bob Dylan. Both artists shared liberal politics and slightly off-key voices. Rodríguez gained a worldwide following and maintained a loyal fan base into the twenty-first century.

In 1973 the government of Chile began to censor the nueva canción movement. That year, military leader Augusto Pinochet and the Chilean army took over the government. Pinochet's forces sought out and silenced artists involved with nueva canción. Some artists were arrested. Others were exiled.

Víctor Jara, pictured here in the 1970s, stood up to the Chilean military government.

THE TRAGEDY OF VÍCTOR JARA

Víctor Jara was one of the leading voices of the Nueva Canción Chilena (New Chilean Song) movement. He wrote poems and songs promoting social justice (equal treatment for people of all social classes). Jara's best-known song is "Te Recuerdo Amanda" ("I Remember You Amanda," 1969). In this song, Jara tells the story of two factory workers, a man and a woman. The man is killed after choosing to fight for workers' rights. "Te Recuerdo Amanda" is quiet yet stirring and very personal. Jara even uses the names of his own parents for the main characters, Manuel and Amanda.

Jara felt music was a powerful tool for promoting change: "I am moved more and more by what I see around me, the poverty of my

own country, of Latin America and other countries of the world," he once said. "But I have also seen what love can do, what the strength of a person who is happy can achieve. Because of all this, and because above all I desire peace, I need the wood and strings of my guitar…some verse which opens up the heart like a wound, some line which helps us all to turn from inside ourselves to look out and see the world with new eyes."

After the military takeover of the Chilean government in 1973, Jara was arrested. Members of the new government's military surrounded the university where Jara worked and ordered him to stop singing. Jara refused. Soldiers smashed his hands, then arrested him and tortured him. They ended the ordeal by shooting him to death. Government soldiers also destroyed the master copies of most of Jara's music, hoping to silence him forever.

The horror of what happened to Víctor Jara shocked the world. But it did not silence other artists. Jara became a symbol for the nueva canción movement throughout Latin America, Spain, and Portugal. Surviving Chilean nueva canción artists fled the nation and lived in exile. Meanwhile, artists in countries such as Argentina, Paraguay, and Uruguay continued to live under hostile governments.

SALSA
DOMINATION

The earliest salsa artists were mainly from New York City. They created the first form of Latin music to develop in a non-Latin nation. By the 1970s, salsa was the style of Latin music in the United States. Salsa music, like the food, combines many ingredients for a hot, spicy result. At first many musicians resisted the term salsa. They pointed out that salsa didn't represent any particular Latin American musical style. One famously said, "I'm a musician, not a cook." But in this sense, salsa was truly American. Salsa music often features the Latin rhythms of son, but it also shows the influence of U.S. pop music.

The Golden Age of Salsa began around 1970. As the popularity of the mambo declined, many Latin stars turned to the salsa sound. The most influential Latin record company of the time, Fania of New York City, was quick to embrace it. Fania's founders, Jerry Masucci and Johnny Pacheco, promoted the salsa sound heavily. Fania also put together a huge stable of the style's most popular artists.

Johnny Pacheco is one of the founders of Fania Records. Pacheco was born in the Dominican Republic and promoted Latin music in New York City.

The sounds of salsa changed constantly during the 1970s. Elements of rock and R & B became more present in salsa music. The trademark Cuban beat took a backseat as artists experimented with new arrangements. Fania drove the scene with its famous Fania All-Stars concerts. These concerts featured the greatest salsa artists of the day, including Celia Cruz, Eddie Palmieri, Ray Barretto, Tito Puente, and Héctor Lavoe. But no All-Stars concert was complete without trombone player Willie Colón.

Tito Puente BELOW and Celia Cruz RIGHT appeared onstage during Fania All-Stars concerts throughout the 1970s. Both artists became legends of the salsa musical style.

STARS OF THE GOLDEN AGE

Willie Colón was one of the driving forces behind the salsa movement. Colón was born to Puerto Rican immigrants in 1950. He grew up in the Bronx borough (district) of New York City. A talented musician from an early age, Colón was attracted to Latin sounds. But simply performing traditional styles didn't appeal to him. Life in the Bronx had exposed him to both traditional Latin forms and American pop music.

Colón made the trombone the centerpiece of his music. This was an unusual decision for a pop or a Latin artist. Colón borrowed popular Cuban and South American rhythms to create a distinctly Latin, yet still brand-new, dance sound. In 1968, when he was still a teenager, he released the album **El Malo (The Bad Guy)**. The record introduced the world to Colón's aggressive salsa music.

Willie Colón, performing here in 2002, is a salsa great and a musical risk taker.

the result of a way of approaching music from the Latin American cultural perspective.

—Willie Colón, n.d.

Héctor Lavoe, pictured here in 1981, was a Puerto Rican salsa singer. Like many salsa musicians, he moved to New York City, where he worked with Willie Colón.

The singer Rubén Blades LEFT was born in Panama. In the 1970s, he became part of the New York salsa scene, also teaming up with Willie Colón RIGHT.

Colón worked with many vocalists throughout his career. His songs with singer Héctor Lavoe are some of his most memorable. They include "El Malo" (1968) and "Te Conozco Bacalao" ("I Know You," 1969). Colón remained a force in salsa throughout the 1970s. His socially relevant music inspired pride in Puerto Rican immigrants.

Other salsa stars of the era included vocalists Rubén Blades and Ismael Miranda. The golden age of salsa ended in the late seventies. However, Colón, Blades, and others continued to make critically acclaimed music for years afterward.

JULIO IGLESIAS AND THE LATIN BALLAD

By the late 1970s and the early 1980s, a mellower brand of Latin pop was on the rise. The bolero-inspired Latin ballad began tearing up the charts. The Latin ballad stood in contrast to the festive salsa sound. It was smooth, slow, and dripping with emotion.

In most cases, Latin ballad singers avoided the social messages

LUIS MIGUEL

Julio Iglesias's songs were inspired by the gentle sounds of bolero music. However, they didn't truly fit the traditional bolero style. For that, fans turned to Mexican star Luis Miguel (ABOVE). Miguel burst onto the Mexican pop scene in the early 1980s at the age of eleven. At age fifteen, he won a Grammy for his duet "Me Gustas Tal Como Eres" ("I Like You Just the Way You Are," 1984) with pop star Sheena Easton. During his early twenties, Miguel dedicated himself to the traditional bolero. He almost single-handedly brought the style back into the mainstream. Many consider him the finest male singer in Latin America. Miguel is the only artist to have two Spanish-language albums go platinum (sell more than one million copies) in the United States.

that had fueled nueva canción and salsa. Balladeers often paired love-song lyrics with slowly strummed guitars or orchestra music. Latin ballads were often directed at women. Even so, balladeers such as Luis Miguel, Roberto Carlos, and José José had their share of fans of both genders. Roberto Carlos songs such as "Detalhes" ("Details," 1971) and "Sua Estupidez" ("Stupidity," 1969) became Latin classics.

The brightest light of the Latin ballad style was Julio Iglesias. The Spanish-born singer had been a goalkeeper for the famous Spanish soccer team Real Madrid. However, a 1963 car accident damaged Iglesias's spine and ended his soccer career. As part of his physical therapy, he took up the guitar. The careful movements needed to play the instrument helped Iglesias regain control of his hands. (He had lost full control due to his spinal injury.) Music spoke to Iglesias. He began writing and singing songs. His natural talent became obvious. In 1968 he entered a Spanish song festival with his pop bolero song "La Vida Sigue Igual" ("Life Goes On"). He won first prize.

Iglesias built a loyal fan base throughout Europe in the 1970s. In the 1980s, he became a force in the U.S. music scene. His breakout

Balladeer José José performs in 2011. His career has spanned more than four decades.

Roberto Carlos, pictured here in the 1970s, is a Brazilian balladeer who came to prominence in the 1960s.

hit was 1984's "To All the Girls I've Loved Before." Country star Willie Nelson joined Iglesias on the song. "To All the Girls I've Loved Before" was an example of how the Latin sound could fuse with country music. It rocketed to the top of Billboard's country charts. Iglesias stayed near the top of the Latin music scene for the next three decades. ★

Julio Iglesias LEFT and Willie Nelson RIGHT perform a duet on **The Tonight Show Starring Johnny Carson** in 1984.

MUST DOWNLOAD Playlist

RAY BARRETTO
"El Watusi" ("The Watusi," 1961)

JOE CUBA SEXTET
"Bang Bang" (1966)

CELIA CRUZ
"Guantanamera"
("The Woman from Guantánamo," 1967)

WILLIE COLÓN AND HÉCTOR LAVOE
"El Malo" ("The Bad Guy," 1968),
"Te Conozco Bacalao" ("I Know You," 1969)

VÍCTOR JARA
"Te Recuerdo Amanda"
("I Remember You Amanda," 1969)

SANTANA
"Soul Sacrifice" (1969),
"Oye Como Va" ("Hear How It Goes," 1970)

SILVIO RODRÍGUEZ
"Ojalá" ("I Wish," 1978)

LUIS MIGUEL AND SHEENA EASTON
"Me Gustas Tal Como Eres"
("I Like You Just the Way You Are," 1984)

chapter **3**

Sensations

Gloria Estefan greets
fans during a concert in
Miami, Florida, in 1991.

WHEN IT COMES TO LATIN POP MUSIC IN THE UNITED STATES, ONE NAME STANDS ABOVE ALL OTHERS: GLORIA ESTEFAN.

Estefan is a seven-time Grammy Award winner. She is often called the Queen of Latin Pop.

Estefan was born in Cuba in 1957. Her family moved to the United States a few years later. Estefan's rise to fame began in 1977. That year she joined a band called Miami Sound Machine. The band took part in the salsa trend, but it wasn't strictly a salsa band. Miami Sound Machine embraced all kinds of pop and Latin influences. Its songs blended disco, a style of urban dance music; funk, a rocking style of R & B; and drum-heavy Cuban conga music. The group released album after album of radio-friendly beats.

By the late 1980s, Estefan was all over radio airwaves. Hits including "Dr. Beat" (1984), "Conga" (1985), and "Bad Boy" (1985) made her a crossover star. Miami Sound Machine understood her massive appeal. In 1988 the band changed its name to Gloria Estefan and the Miami Sound Machine. A year later, they dropped the Miami Sound Machine name altogether.

Gloria Estefan and Miami Sound Machine pose before a TV appearance in 1987.

Estefan was at the height of her popularity when disaster struck. In March 1990, she was on tour supporting her smash album **Cuts Both Ways** (1989) when a semitruck crashed into her tour bus. Estefan was badly hurt and nearly died. Doctors had to put two titanium rods into her spine, which had been crushed in the accident. She spent more than a year in physical therapy and made a full recovery.

The accident sparked a change in Estefan's music. Starting with 1991's **Into the Light**, she explored more traditional styles. She released the Latin ballad "Coming out of the Dark" (1991) in both English and in Spanish. It was another hit, reaching No. 1 on Billboard's Hot 100 chart. Estefan has continued to evolve since then, both as an artist and a producer.

THE RISE OF
MERENGUE

Merengue made a surprise splash in the U.S. pop scene during the 1980s. The music had long been popular in the Dominican Republic, Haiti, and Venezuela. It emerged from the folk music of working people in these countries. In the early twentieth century, musicians such as the Dominican bandleader Ñico Lora developed the modern merengue sound.

Merengue is fast-paced dancing music. The music's early folk form relied mostly on string

Local musicians perform with traditional merengue instruments in the Dominican Republic.

instruments. The traditional merengue features three instruments: an accordion, a *tambora* (a double-headed drum), and a *güira* (a percussion instrument similar to a guiro). Merengue lyrics and the dancing that goes with them are often sexually suggestive.

The merengue style had enjoyed minor success in the United States in the 1950s. Merengue band Angel Viloria y Su Conjunto Típico Cibaeño scored stateside hits such as "A Lo Oscuro" ("In the Dark," 1951).

But it really took off in the late 1980s. By the 1990s, most merengue groups had added a saxophone and a bass guitar to the mix.

The artist most responsible for merengue's popularity was Juan Luis Guerra. Like merengue's pioneers, Guerra was a native of the Dominican Republic. In 1984 he formed the band Juan Luis Guerra y 440 (often called Grupo 440). Guerra brought powerful lyrics to the core merengue sound. He and his bandmates often spiced songs up with African and Brazilian twists. Guerra became a huge star in Latin America.

In 1990 the Guerra–Grupo 440 song "Ojalá Que Llueva Café"

("I Hope It Rains Coffee") was featured in a coffee commercial. It won the band international attention. Later that year, Grupo 440 took advantage of its fame with the release of the album ***Bachata Rosa (Pink Spree)***. The album won a Grammy Award for Best Tropical Latin Performance, the first such honor to go to a merengue group. Since then many other talented merengue artists have emerged from the genre, including Elvis Crespo and Quezada.

TEJANO
MUSIC

Texas shares a long border with Mexico, its neighbor to the south. The two places share a long history too. Texans with Mexican roots often refer to themselves as Tejanos (from Tejas, the Spanish word for Texas). Tejanos have had their own musical styles for more than a century.

Juan Luis Guerra, pictured here in 2004, helped revive interest in merengue music across the United States.

THE MARIACHI

One of the best known Mexican musical styles is mariachi. The guitar and the *guitarrón* (bass guitar) drive mariachi music. Mariachi bands also feature violins, trumpets, and sometimes even a harp. These bands are famous for their fancy cowboy style of dress.

Mariachi music began in western Mexico in the 1800s. By the 1930s, the music had moved east, to Mexico City. Mariachi groups began adding horns to their music around this time. Although mariachi music has a unique sound, it has had little influence on pop music in the United States. However, some artists in Mexico have enjoyed popular success. **Alejandro Fernández** (LEFT) is a Mexican chart topper with a modern take on mariachi on albums such as *Que Seas Muy Feliz* (*Very Last Moment*, 1995). The U.S. punk-rock band the Bronx has released two mariachi albums under the name **Mariachi el Bronx** (RIGHT), *Mariachi el Bronx Vol. 1 and Vol. 2* (2009, 2011).

Tejano music (or Tex-Mex) is Latin at its core. Performers often sing its songs in Spanish or in a combination of Spanish and English. It draws from European waltzes and polkas as well as rock, jazz, and country. This blend allows Tejanos to embrace both U.S. culture and Mexican heritage.

By the 1980s, Tejano included all sorts of styles. Tejano musicians performed everything from sweet ballads to stirring dance music.

Perhaps the best-known Tejano style is conjunto. The conjunto sound relies on a few core instruments. They include an accordion, a bajo sexto, an electric bass guitar, and drums. The accordion, a German import, may seem like a strange addition to the Tejano sound. But many German workers traveled to northern Mexico in the late 1800s looking for industrial jobs. Some brought their accordions. The very different sounds came together to form a one-of-a-kind hybrid.

Although Tejano music has been around a long time, it didn't really achieve widespread success until the 1980s. A big part of that success was innovative accordion player Jaime de Anda and his band Los Chamacos (The Kids). Their albums...**No Se Cansan** (...**Don't Get Tired**, 1996) and **Conjunto Power** (2003) were each nominated for a Grammy.

Jaime de Anda and Los Chamacos (or Jaime y Los Chamacos) stop to pose at the 2009 Latin Grammys. This group won fans in the United States and Mexico with its modern take on Tejano music.

SPANGLISH

For many decades, most Latin American performers sang only in Spanish or Portuguese. The lyrics of songs were sung in translation for English-speaking markets or simply released in Spanish, as with Ritchie Valens's "La Bamba" (1958). However, songs that blend both languages have become more common in recent years. In songs such as Enrique Iglesias's "Bailamos" ("Let's Dance," 1999), singers switch back and forth between languages mid-verse. This mix of English and Spanish is often called Spanglish. Spanglish lyrics have become a staple of the modern Latin pop scene.

THE SELENA SENSATION

In the late 1980s, an exciting new artist gave the Tejano music scene a huge boost. Selena Quintanilla-Pérez (or simply Selena) was a Texas teenager with a lovable stage presence and a voice like few others. Selena's father had been a musician. He pushed his children in the same direction. Young Selena was his shining star.

In 1984 Selena released her first album, **Mis Primeras Grabaciones (My First Recordings)**. She was thirteen. Three years later, she won the title of Performer of the Year at the Tejano Music Awards. Like many Latin stars before her, Selena was not content to reproduce classic Latin sounds. She had grown up listening to American pop. She infused her music with electronic sounds and modern dance beats.

By the early 1990s, Selena was the most popular Tejano musician in the world. Adoring fans followed her every move. Her 1992 album **Entre a Mi Mundo (Enter My World)** was a critical and popular success. It brought in pop fans from beyond the Tejano community. The album featured one of her biggest hits, "Como La Flor" ("Like the Flower"). The song became a worldwide success.

As she reached her twenties, Selena continued to push the boundaries of Latin music. In 1994 Selena revealed a new sound with the release of her album **Amor Prohibido (Forbidden Love)**. The album featured a unique fusion of Tejano, salsa, funk, R & B, and hip-hop. She focused more than ever on English lyrics. Her new style could be heard in hits such as "Techno Cumbia." Selena also covered the Pretenders' rock hit "Back on the Chain Gang" (1982), which she retitled "Fotos y Recuerdos" ("Photos and Memories").

Selena's new sound was designed to appeal to a wider audience. But **Amor Prohibido** was a smash with her longtime fans too. It seemed that Selena was on her way toward achieving her dream of becoming the first Tejano megastar.

Selena lets loose at a concert in 1995.

> If you listen to our past albums...you can tell we grew up listening to English and Spanish.
>
> Our sound isn't so hardcore Tex-Mex or Mexican....One of the keys to our success is that we're different.
>
> It doesn't sound traditional.

—Selena, 1995

DEVASTATING

In 1995 Selena was hard at work on her next album, *Dreaming of You*. The album's songs continued what she had started with *Amor Prohibido*. In March of that year, Selena and her family learned that the president of her fan club, Yolanda Saldívar, was stealing money from them. They fired Saldívar.

On March 31, Selena met with Saldívar at a Texas motel. She hoped to recover financial records that Saldívar had kept. But Saldívar was in no mood for a discussion. Instead, Saldívar pulled out a gun and shot the twenty-three-year-old star in the right shoulder. Selena rushed to the motel lobby for help, but emergency workers could not get to the motel in time. She died from blood loss.

BUENA VISTA SOCIAL CLUB

In the late 1990s, traditional Cuban music made a big comeback in the United States. The Cuban music revival was all thanks to the Latin supergroup **Buena Vista Social Club**. The band was named for a popular Cuban music club from the first half of the twentieth century. It featured twenty of Cuba's biggest music stars of the 1940s and the 1950s. Members included guitarist and vocalist **Juan de Marcos González** (TOP), pianist **Rubén González** (SECOND FROM TOP), and bassist **Orlando "Cachaito" López** (THIRD FROM TOP).

Buena Vista Social Club played traditional Cuban music, including son, bolero, and rumba. According to group founder Juan de Marcos González, the group created songs "that serve as a symbol of the power of Cuban music, and which . . . have contributed to Cuban music regaining the status it always had in Latin American and world music."

Los Angeles–born guitarist **Ry Cooder** (BOTTOM) gathered the musicians together in 1996. In 1997 Buena Vista Social Club released an album of the same name. The release hit No. 1 on the *Billboard* World Music and Latin Music charts. A 1999 film by German filmmaker Wim Wenders featured performances by the group. The movie received an Oscar nomination for Best Documentary.

Selena's death devastated fans of Latin pop music. Texas governor George W. Bush declared Selena's birthday, April 16, Selena Day in Texas. **Dreaming of You** was released in July of 1995. The album debuted at No. 1 on the U.S. Billboard Hot 100 chart. Selena became the first Latin artist to accomplish that feat. The album sold more than two million copies in its first year. It remains one of the best-selling female pop albums of all time.

Selena's death drew more attention to the Latin music scene in the United States. So did Selena (1997), a film about her life starring Jennifer Lopez as Selena. Stateside listeners were starting to realize that Latin music did not belong on the edges of pop. People of Latin descent were making up a bigger and bigger portion of the U.S. music audience. Other music fans were checking out Latin sounds as well. Exciting new Latin stars were trying to fill the role that Selena left behind. A major change was coming to pop, and it was coming with a salsa beat. ★

Jennifer Lopez performs in a scene from the 1997 film **Selena**.

♪ MUST DOWNLOAD *Playlist*

MIAMI SOUND MACHINE
"Bad Boy" (1985),
"Conga" (1985)

JUAN LUIS GUERRA Y 440
"Ojalá Que Llueva Café"
("I Hope It Rains Coffee,"
1990)

LOS LOBOS
"The Neighborhood" (1990)

GLORIA ESTEFAN
"Coming out of the Dark"
(1991)

SELENA
"Como La Flor" ("Like the
Flower," 1992),
"Fotos y Recuerdos"
("Photos and Memories,"
1994)

ALEJANDRO FERNÁNDEZ
"Como Quien Pierde una
Estrella" ("As Star of the
Show," 1995)

JAIME Y LOS CHAMACOS
"Yolanda" (1996)

**BUENA VISTA SOCIAL
CLUB**
"Chan Chan" (1997)

chapter 4

THE LATIN Explosion

Ricky Martin dances during a 1999 concert, at the peak of the Latin Explosion.

AS THE CALENDAR TURNED TO 1999, LATIN MUSIC HAD FOUND A PLACE IN THE U.S. POP MUSIC SCENE.

But it remained a niche (small segment). Attitudes were changing, however. Selena had proved that listeners were more open than ever to Latin sounds. A new star was about to finish what she had started.

Ricky Martin (Enrique Martin Morales) was a former child star from Puerto Rico. In the 1980s, he had spent five years in the Puerto Rican boy band Menudo. After leaving the group in 1989, Martin faded from fame. He pursued an acting career for a time and released Spanish-only albums to Latin markets. His 1995 album *A Medio Vivir (Half Living)* enjoyed some international praise—just not in the United States.

All of that changed in 1999. That year, Martin released his first English-language album, *Ricky Martin*. The first single off the album was a salsa-inspired tune called "Livin' La Vida Loca" ("Livin' the Crazy Life"). The song kicked off a movement that changed the face of pop music in the United States.

GOING CRAZY

With "Livin' La Vida Loca," Ricky Martin became an overnight star in

Ricky Martin FAR LEFT and other members of the boy band Menudo goof around in 1987.

the United States. The song's Spanglish lyrics were easy to learn and fun to sing along with. Its upbeat tempo got people shaking their hips. And Martin was the perfect star: young, good-looking, and with a flair for showmanship. He had the dance moves to back up his music. Soon his face was showing up on magazine covers and TV screens.

"Livin' La Vida Loca" rocketed up the Billboard Hot 100 chart, spending five weeks in the top spot. It also reached No. 1 in many other countries, from Canada to the United Kingdom to New Zealand. Near the end of 1999, the video for "Livin' La Vida Loca" took home the Best Dance Video and Best Pop Video honors at the MTV Video Music Awards. In 2000 **Ricky Martin** was nominated for a Grammy Award, Best Pop Vocal. It was official—Ricky Martin was the crossover sensation fans of Latin pop had been waiting for.

Martin was far from the only artist to benefit from the success of "Livin' La Vida Loca." The song triggered the Latin Explosion in the pop music world. Suddenly record companies were scrambling to sign Latin talent. Within months, artists such as Jennifer Lopez, Enrique Iglesias, and Marc Anthony were filling the airwaves with their own Latin beats.

LATIN POP PRINCESS

Some people compared the Latin Explosion to the British Invasion of the 1960s. During the British Invasion, bands from the United Kingdom such as the Beatles and the Who scored hit after hit on the U.S. music charts. However, there was no invasion during the Latin Explosion. Many of the top names in modern Latin music are U.S. citizens.

New York City native Jennifer Lopez was one of the first artists to step through the door that Ricky Martin opened. Lopez had started her show-business career as a dancer in the early 1990s. She showed off her moves on the TV show In Living Color and worked as a background dancer for pop star Janet Jackson. In the mid-1990s, Lopez turned her attention to acting. Her roles in films such as My Family (1995) and Money Train (1995) earned her acclaim. Her star rose higher when she played

Many of **Ricky Martin**'s hit songs are about love and relationships. Even so, Martin had been reluctant to talk about his sexuality in the years surrounding the Latin Explosion. But in 2010, Ricky Martin became Latin music's biggest openly gay male star. In a March 29, 2010, post on his website, Martin declared that he was "proud to say that I am a fortunate homosexual man." Later that year, Martin released his autobiography, Me. The best-selling book gave fans an even closer look into Martin's private life.

Jennifer Lopez shows off her moves during a 2001 performance in New York City. Lopez has become a star across music, film, TV, and fashion.

the title role in the 1997 film *Selena*. Lopez won an American Latino Media Arts Award (ALMA) for the performance. Critics praised both her acting and her singing in the film. In 1999 Lopez made a push to become a pop star.

At first some people compared Lopez's career to that of Selena. Lopez bristled at such comparisons. "Selena had the ability to do the crossover thing because she was singing in Spanish," Lopez pointed out. "I have never acted in a Spanish movie. I was born in the Bronx. 'Crossover' is when you cross over from one market to another. I've always been in this market."

Lopez's first album, **On the 6** (1999), reached *Billboard's* top ten. She had successfully crossed over from acting to pop music. **On the 6** had heavy doses of R & B and hip-hop, and most of her lyrics were in English. But over time, Lopez embraced more Latin sounds, especially those of salsa. In 2007 she released the Spanish-language album **Como Ama una Mujer (As a Woman Loves)**.

Throughout the 2000s, Lopez continued to release hit records while maintaining an acting career. She was even named *People* magazine's Sexiest Woman Alive in 2011. With each successful album and film, she further cemented her place as a pop icon.

LATIN HERITAGE, POP SOUNDS

What makes an artist a Latin artist? The line can be blurry. Is simply being of Latin descent enough? Some fans argue that artists such as Jennifer Lopez aren't really Latin artists at all. They're pop artists who happen to be Latin Americans.

Selena Gomez (LEFT) and Demi Lovato (RIGHT) are two singers of Mexican heritage. Both Gomez and Lovato were born in the United States. In recent years, both have also exploded in popularity. Many listeners would say that their music is straightforward pop, not Latin pop. In many ways, these young artists are following in the footsteps of Lopez. Their songs are inspired by other artists, such as Katy Perry or Rihanna, whose music teenagers and preteens enjoy.

ENRIQUE IGLESIAS AND THE
NEW LATIN BALLAD

As a teenager, Enrique Iglesias didn't want to take advantage of the fame of his father, the legendary Julio Iglesias. Enrique didn't even tell his dad about his plans to break into music. Instead, he borrowed money and produced his earliest recordings under the name Enrique Martinez.

Enrique's famous last name did eventually come in handy. In the mid-1990s, he began recording under his own name. He quickly built a fan base in Latin America. Hits such as "Si Tú Te Vas" ("If You Go," 1995) fueled his rise to success. Although Enrique didn't have the natural raw vocal power or range of his father, his silky-smooth vocals and natural good looks gave fans plenty of reason to swoon.

Enrique believed that true artists wrote most of their own music. He worked as hard at his writing as he did at his performances. His hard work paid off in 1999. Enrique's song "Bailamos" ("Let's Dance") soared to No. 1 on the Billboard Hot 100. Suddenly, Iglesias was a star in the United States. U.S. record companies launched a bidding war to sign the young up-and-comer. Iglesias signed a contract for $50 million with Universal Music Group. His first English-language release was *Enrique* (1999). It sold more than ten million copies worldwide.

In the years after the Latin Explosion, many Latin artists enjoyed a hit or two, then flamed out. Not so with Iglesias. His second album, 2001's *Escape*, was an even bigger hit than *Enrique*. It included such hits as "Escape" and "Don't Turn Off the Lights." One of Iglesias's most interesting projects was 2010's *Euphoria*. This bilingual album sidestepped the practice of releasing English-only, Spanish-only, or Spanglish albums. Instead, *Euphoria* features seven songs in English and six in Spanish.

Enrique Iglesias performs for fans in 2002.

THE NEW FACE OF SALSA

The Latin Explosion ushered in a wide range of new artists and styles. Salsa music also crowned a new king: Marc Anthony.

Marc Anthony was born Marco Antonio Muñiz in 1968 in New York City. His parents named him after Mexican singer Marco Antonio Solís. When he decided to pursue a career in music, Anthony changed his name to avoid confusion with his famous namesake. Anthony began his career as a songwriter and background vocalist working for such groups as Menudo and the Latin Rascals. In the early 1990s, Anthony decided to focus on salsa. The decision would lead him to stardom. But stardom didn't happen right away. Anthony focused on Spanish language music at first. His second Spanish album, *Todo a Su Tiempo (Everything in Its Time)*, earned him Billboard's award for Hot Tropical Artist of the Year. Even so, he remained unknown among pop fans.

In 1999 Anthony released his first English-language album since 1991. *Marc Anthony* (1999) climbed to No. 8 on the *Billboard* album chart. The HBO television network broadcast one of his concerts, and

I'm not a salsa singer who wants to sing in English, and I'm not this American kid who wants to sing Spanish. My thing is music, period.

his song "You Sang to Me" (2000) was heard in the film comedy *Runaway Bride*. Throughout the following decade, Anthony released one dance-friendly salsa album after the next. He also was married to Jennifer Lopez for a time, began an acting career, and became a full-blown celebrity. Through it all, he stayed true to his roots. No artist has done more to bring salsa back to the mainstream.

CHRISTINA AGUILERA AND THE REVERSE CROSSOVER

Most Latin American crossover stars turned Spanish-language success into English-language stardom. The opposite was the case with Christina Aguilera.

Aguilera's father is from Ecuador, but she was born in New York City. She began her career as a child star, performing on the TV show *The Mickey Mouse Club* alongside Ryan Gosling and Justin Timberlake. In 1998, at the age of seventeen, she found musical success with her song "Reflection" for the animated film *Mulan*. The song earned Aguilera a Golden Globe nomination. The next year, Aguilera released her first album, **Christina Aguilera** (1999). The album soared to the top of the charts on the strength of singles such as "Genie in a Bottle," "What a Girl Wants," and "Come On Over Baby (All I Want Is You)."

Aguilera had become a pop star, but she wanted to honor her Latin heritage. In 2000 she released a Spanish-language album—despite the fact that she didn't speak Spanish. The album, **Mi Reflejo (My Reflection)**, included six new songs as well as five songs from **Christina Aguilera** translated into Spanish. Aguilera ruled the Latin charts just as she had the pop charts. **Mi Reflejo** won her the Latin Grammy for Best Female Pop Vocal Album. Aguilera later returned to TV as a judge on the singing contest **The Voice**.

Christina Aguilera belts out a hit in 2000. Aguilera celebrated her Ecuadorian heritage on the album **Mi Reflejo** (2000).

SHAKIRA'S FRESH SOUNDS

While artists like Marc Anthony embrace tradition, musicians such as Shakira Ripoll (known as Shakira) blaze new trails. Shakira's unique style mixes Latin, Middle Eastern, and rock sounds. She reached the peak of pop music in the years following the Latin Explosion. Shakira may be the most influential Latin artist of the modern era—even if her music fails to fall neatly into the category of Latin, pop, rock, or folk.

Born in Colombia to Lebanese parents, Shakira grew up hearing the sounds of the Middle East as well as those of Latin America. She signed her first record contract at age thirteen and never looked back. Unlike many teen stars, Shakira had little interest in cranking out bubblegum (easy-listening teen) pop. Instead, she created her own sound. Her songs blended pop, rock, folk, and Caribbean music. They had edgy lyrics that in many ways carried on the nueva canción tradition.

Shakira was a superstar among Spanish-speaking audiences before the Latin Explosion. In 2001 she introduced herself to the United States with a bang. Many crossover artists who are native Spanish speakers rely on songwriters to create their English material. But Shakira learned English in order to write lyrics in the language. The result was her first English-heavy album, **Laundry Service** (2001). Her fresh sound spoke to U.S. audiences who were bored with the same old styles. The album's first single, "Whenever, Wherever," became the top-selling song of 2002.

Over the next ten years, Shakira continued to experiment with new sounds. She released albums both in English and Spanish. Her 2009 release, **She Wolf**, featured the song "Waka Waka (This Time for Africa)." The song was chosen as the official song of soccer's 2010 World Cup, giving Shakira a new level of worldwide popularity.

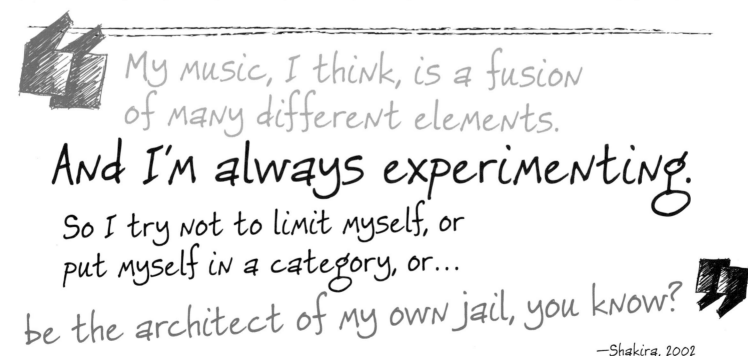

My music, I think, is a fusion of many different elements. And I'm always experimenting. So I try not to limit myself, or put myself in a category, or... be the architect of my own jail, you know?

—Shakira, 2002

Shakira performs "Waka Waka (This Time for Africa)" at the 2010 World Cup kickoff celebration in South Africa.

LATIN ROCK
LIVES ON

Ballads and dance-friendly pop tunes may dominate Latin pop music, but rock 'n' roll fans have plenty of choices as well. The same year the Latin Explosion took place, Carlos Santana made a massive comeback. His album *Supernatural* (1999) featured guest stars such as Dave Matthews and Cee Lo Green. The album's song "Smooth," written and sung by Rob Thomas of Matchbox 20, became a No. 1 hit. Both *Supernatural* and "Smooth" won multiple Grammy Awards.

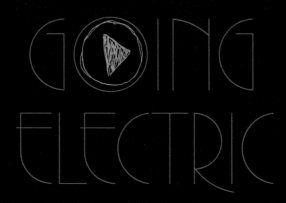

GOING ELECTRIC

Latin music has always been closely linked to dancing. So it's no surprise that it has linked up with electronic music. Many popular electronic musicians use computers and synthesizers to make music for dancing. Electronic music typically has a strong, pounding beat and gets heavy play in dance clubs. One of the most popular styles of Latin-inspired electronic music is bossa electronica. This spin on bossa nova music combines the cool, lyrical style of the bossa nova with modern electronic sounds.

The song "Smooth," by Rob Thomas LEFT helped Santana RIGHT cross over in 1999.

Los Lonely Boys have found success with a bluesy sound they call Texican Rock 'n' Roll. The band is made up of three brothers from San Angelo, Texas. Henry Garza sings and plays guitar, while Ringo Garza drums and Jojo Garza plays bass. Their first single, "Heaven" (2004), reached the top spot on Billboard's Adult Contemporary chart.

Fans rave about the band's energetic live show.

Rodrigo y Gabriela (Rodrigo Sánchez and Gabriela Quintero) take fans back to a time when much of Latin music was instrumental. Their folk rock formula is simple: two acoustic guitars and some simple percussion instruments. Sánchez plays lead parts and Quintero

plays rhythm guitar. Songs such as "Tamacun" (2006) re-create the classic sound of the Spanish guitar. In 2010 Rodrigo y Gabriela had the chance to play for U.S. president Barack Obama.

Latin rockers have found success with other styles as well. Zach de la Rocha is a California-born rapper of Latino heritage. He has

Texican Rock 'n' Roll stars
Los Lonely Boys lay down a
groove in California in 2004.

made his voice heard as part of the fierce rap-rock group Rage Against the Machine. Fans of heavy metal can turn to Brazilian heavy-metal rockers Sepultura or Mexico's Transmetal. Peru is home to legendary punk bands such as Leusemia and Dolores Delirio.

Zach de la Rocha LEFT is the lead rapper for the politically charged band Rage Against the Machine.

HIP-HOP AND REGGAETON

In recent years, the Latin beat has made a bigger and bigger impact on hip-hop music. Artists such as the rapper Pitbull (Armando Pérez) celebrate their Latin roots. Pitbull was born in Miami to Cuban immigrant parents. With his beat-heavy style, he has turned out hit after hit, including 2011's "Give Me Everything" and "International Love." Other influential Latin hip-hop

artists include Mellow Man Ace (Ulpiano Reyes), Immortal Technique (Felipe Coronel), and the Cuban crew Orishas.

Reggaeton music fuses hip-hop sounds with reggae. Reggae is a rhythmic form of music native to the English-speaking Caribbean

nation of Jamaica. Reggaeton's combination of reggae and hip-hop is also popular among Latin American musicians and fans. Wisin and Yandel (Juan Luis Morera Luna and Llandel Veguilla Malavé) are among the most successful reggaeton groups. The duo

AMERICANIZATION

The impact of Latin music on U.S. pop is undeniable. But it may pale in comparison to the effect American styles have had in Latin America. Much of current popular music in Latin America takes after the rock, pop, and hip-hop styles of the United States. This trend is known as the Americanization of Latin American music. While many fans welcome the blend of sounds, others worry that young people are losing touch with their culture—and becoming Americanized. These critics say that traditional musical forms have been replaced by styles with little social value and few links to Latin American history.

started making music in their native Puerto Rico. They drew in both Spanish- and English-speaking audiences with hits such as "Me Estás Tentando" ("You're Tempting Me," 2008) and "Follow the Leader," a 2012 collaboration with Jennifer Lopez. In 2012 Wisin and Yandel proved how popular reggaeton had become by taking home the MTV Video Music Award (VMA) for Best Latino Artist. Other popular reggaeton artists include Daddy Yankee (Ramón Luis Ayala Rodríguez) and Don Omar (William Omar Rivera).

THE FUTURE OF
LATIN MUSIC

Latin music has come a long way in the United States—and the world—over the past century. Latin American styles evolved from their traditional forms, merged with North American pop sounds, and transformed the landscape of pop music everywhere. Even thirty years ago, few people could have imagined how quickly Latin sounds would change—and be changed by—American pop.

In the twenty-first century, it can be difficult to separate Latin music from American pop. Often the only difference between a Latin song and a pop song is the heritage of the singer, or the use of Spanish or Spanglish lyrics. So what's next for Latin music? Latin sounds will certainly continue to influence American pop. And the opposite is true as well. Styles from the United States and around the world have been influencing music in Latin America just as much. Will the line between pop and Latin music get blurrier? Or will some Latin artists return to traditional forms? It's hard to guess what the future holds. But fans can be sure that the future of pop music in America will have a Latin tinge. ★

MUST DOWNLOAD Playlist

RAGE AGAINST THE MACHINE
"Bulls on Parade" (1996)

ENRIQUE IGLESIAS
"Bailamos" ("Let's Dance," 1999)

MARC ANTHONY
"I Need to Know" (1999)

JENNIFER LOPEZ
"If You Had My Love" (1999)

RICKY MARTIN
"Livin' La Vida Loca" ("Livin' the Crazy Life," 1999)

SANTANA FEAT. ROB THOMAS
"Smooth" (1999)

SHAKIRA
"Whenever, Wherever" (2001)

LOS LONELY BOYS
"Heaven" (2004)

RODRIGO Y GABRIELA
"Tamacun" (2006)

PITBULL
"Give Me Everything" (2011)

WISIN AND YANDEL FEAT. JENNIFER LOPEZ
"Follow the Leader" (2012)

GLOSSARY

ballad: a slow song that tells a story. Ballads often have sorrowful or romantic lyrics.

bilingual: able to speak two languages. In music, an album is considered bilingual if it includes songs in two different languages.

bolero: a lyrically driven style of Cuban ballad

bossa nova: a laid-back version of samba music, often accompanied by nothing but a guitar. Bossa nova originated in Brazil.

crossover star: a musician who has successfully moved from one musical style to another

fusion: a combination of two or more elements or styles

mambo: a style of Cuban dance music famous for its strong beat and flowing style

merengue: a style of fast-paced dancing music with roots in the Dominican Republic

nueva canción: a politically driven form of Latin folk music from the 1960s and 1970s, through which artists often spoke out against war and government oppression

percussion: a class of instruments that are played by striking with the hand, finger, or other object, or by shaking them. Drums are a well-known percussion instrument.

rumba: an upbeat form of Cuban dance music famous for its call-and-response vocal pattern

salsa: a style of Latin music that originated in the United States. Salsa blends Latin sounds with U.S. pop, rock, R & B, and other styles and is popular as dance music.

samba: a style of Brazilian party music that evolved from the folk songs of Brazilians with African heritage

sexteto: a band consisting of six members

son: a traditional form of Cuban folk music featuring a Spanish flavor and an African beat

Spanglish: an informal combination of English and Spanish

syncopation: the stressing of a beat that is not normally stressed or the skipping of a beat that is normally stressed. Syncopation is a staple of many styles of music, including Latin.

tango: a style of instrumental dance music from Argentina

tango canción: a version of the tango with lyrics, created by Carlos Gardel in the 1910s

Tejano: a Mexican American resident of Texas or a musical style popularized by people of this background. Tejano music has a polkalike beat inspired by the music of German immigrants to this part of the United States.

TIMELINE

1868 Cuba wins independence from Spain. Cuban soldiers gather in Havana and help to create the modern son sound.

1910s Trío Matamoros brings the son sound out of Cuba, introducing it to audiences in the United States and around the world.

1917 Carlos Gardel unveils his tango canción style at a concert in Buenos Aires, Argentina. The new sound later becomes a success in the United States.

1950s The United States—especially New York City—experiences mambo mania. Desi Arnaz, Pérez Prado, and others score stateside hits.

1958 Ritchie Valens releases the Spanish-language rock song "La Bamba." The song helps to launch the Latin rock genre.

1959 Fidel Castro and the Communist Party come to power in Cuba, cutting off many Cuban Americans from their homeland. These musicians begin to develop their own sound, which later is called salsa.

1964 Astrud Gilberto, João Gilberto, and Stan Getz release "The Girl from Ipanema." The song sets off a bossa nova craze in the United States.

1970 The period known as the Golden Age of Salsa begins.

1973 Chilean musician Víctor Jara is arrested and then killed by the Chilean government for his socially conscious music. He becomes a symbol for the politically charged nueva canción movement.

1977 Gloria Estefan joins the Miami Sound Machine.

1984 Tejano star Selena releases her first album, Mis Primeras Grabaciones (My First Recordings)

1995 Selena is shot and killed by the former president of her fan club.

1999 Ricky Martin's "Livin' La Vida Loca" ("Livin' the Crazy Life") sets off a movement known as the Latin Explosion.

2010 Shakira's song "Waka Waka (This Time for Africa)" is selected as the official song of the 2010 World Cup. The choice gives Latin music a worldwide boost in popularity.

2011 Jennifer Lopez wins Favorite Latin Artist at the American Music Awards.

MINI BIOS

Rubén Blades (born 1948): Rubén Blades was born Rubén Blades Bellido de Luna in Panama City, Panama. He helped bring the political messages of nueva canción to U.S. salsa music. He became a salsa star in the 1970s and the 1980s. His popular songs include "Pedro Navaja" ("Pedro Razor," 1978) and "El Cantante" ("The Singer," 1978). In 1994 he ran for the Panamanian presidency and lost. In 2004 he was made Panama's minister of tourism.

Willie Colón (born 1950): The trombonist Willie Colón was born in New York City to Puerto Rican immigrant parents. Colón was perhaps the biggest salsa star of the 1970s. He signed with Fania Records at age fifteen and released his first album two years later. Colón was famous for blending a range of styles. He had many successful collaborations with other salsa stars. He is also an actor, music producer, and political activist.

Gloria Estefan (born 1957): Gloria Estefan is known as the Queen of Latin Pop. Estefan was born in Havana, Cuba, but soon moved to Miami, Florida. She joined the band Miami Sound Machine in 1977 and went on to become one of the biggest Latin pop stars in history. In 1990 her tour bus was struck by a semitruck, causing severe injuries to her spine. She survived and has continued to thrive as an artist and a music producer.

Carlos Gardel (1890–1935): Born in Toulouse, France, Carlos Gardel moved to Argentina at the age of two. He created the tango canción in 1917, adding lyrics to the normally instrumental tango. The new style created a worldwide sensation. He died in a plane crash in 1935, at the height of his popularity.

João Gilberto (born 1931): Born in Juazeiro, Brazil, João Gilberto is credited with creating the smooth sound of the bossa nova. Gilberto started playing guitar at age fourteen. He tried to make it as a samba vocalist before turning his full attention to guitar. The sounds of American jazz led him to create a new sound, bossa nova. His most famous recording is "The Girl from Ipanema" (1964), with Astrud Gilberto and Stan Getz.

Ricky Martin (born 1971): Ricky Martin was born Enrique Martín Morales in San Juan, Puerto Rico. Martin joined the Puerto Rican boy band Menudo in 1984 and remained a member until 1989. For the next decade, he was a Spanish-language star and actor. Martin's 1999 pop song "Livin' La Vida Loca" ("Livin' the Crazy Life") ignited the Latin Explosion.

Carmen Miranda (1909–1955): Carmen Miranda was born in Marco de Canaveses, Portugal. She became one of the most famous samba singers of her time. Miranda rose to fame in Brazil in the 1930s and then found stardom in music and films in the United States in the 1940s and early the 1950s.

Pitbull (born 1981): Armando Pérez was born in Miami, Florida, to Cuban parents. When he began a career in hip-hop, he took the name Pitbull. Early on, he impressed fans with guest verses on songs by the rapper Lil Jon in 2002. Pitbull later became a superstar with hits such as "Give Me Everything" (2011) and his team-up with Jennifer Lopez, "On the Floor" (2011).

Shakira (born 1977): Shakira Isabel Mebarak Ripoll, born in Barranquilla, Colombia, may be the most influential Latin star of her era. Her music blends Latin, Middle Eastern, and rock styles. She signed her first record contract at age thirteen and became a huge Spanish-language star. In the late 1990s, she learned English and crossed over to become a full-blown pop sensation. Her famous songs include "Whenever, Wherever" (2001) and "Hips Don't Lie" (2005).

LATIN MUST-HAVES

Must-Have Albums

Ritchie Valens, *Ritchie Valens* (1959)

Stan Getz and João Gilberto, *Getz/Gilberto* (1964)

Willie Colón, *El Malo (The Bad Guy,* 1967)

Ray Barretto, *Acid* (1968)

Santana, *Santana* (1969)

Fania All-Stars, *Live at the Cheetah,* Vol. 1 (1972)

Silvio Rodríguez, *Días y Flores (Days and Flowers,* 1975)

Rubén Blades and Willie Colón, *Siembra (Sowing,* 1978)

Julio Iglesias, *1100 Bel Air Place* (1984)

Gloria Estefan, *Cuts Both Ways* (1990)

Selena, *Dreaming of You* (1995)

Buena Vista Social Club, *Buena Vista Social Club* (1997)

Marc Anthony, *Marc Anthony* (1999)

Santana, *Supernatural* (1999)

Celia Cruz, *Celia Cruz and Friends: A Night of Salsa* (2000)

Enrique Iglesias, *Escape* (2001)

Shakira, *Laundry Service* (2001)

Jamie y Los Chamacos, *Conjunto Power* (2003)

Mana, *Drama y Luz (Drama and Light,* 2011)

Wisin and Yandel, *Los Vaqueros: El Regreso (The Cowboys: The Return,* 2011)

Ximena Sariñana, *Ximena Sariñana* (2011)

Rodrigo y Gabriela, *Area 52* (2012)

Must-Have Songs

Rita Montaner, "El Manicero" ("The Peanut Vendor," 1928)

Carmen Miranda, "I, Yi, Yi, Yi, Yi (I Like You Very Much)" (1941)

Desi Arnaz, "El Cumbanchero" ("The Brave Combo," 1949)

Beny Moré, "Bonito y Sabroso" ("Beautiful and Tasty," 1952)

Pérez Prado, "Cereza Rosa" ("Cherry Pink," 1955)

Ray Barretto, "El Watusi" ("The Watusi," 1961)

Stan Getz, Astrud Gilberto, and João Gilberto, "The Girl from Ipanema" (1964)

Joe Cuba Sextet, "Bang Bang" (1966)

Willie Colón & Héctor Lavoe, "El Malo" ("The Bad Guy," 1967)

Celia Cruz, "Guantanamera" ("The Woman from Guantánamo," 1967)

Víctor Jara, "Te Recuerdo Amanda" ("I Remember You Amanda," 1969)

Santana, "Soul Sacrifice" (1969)

Miami Sound Machine, "Conga" (1985)

Juan Luis Guerra y 440, "Ojalá Que Llueva Café" ("I Hope It Rains Coffee," 1990)

Selena, "Fotos y Recuerdos" ("Photos and Memories," 1994)

Buena Vista Social Club, "Chan Chan" (1997)

Marc Anthony, "I Need to Know" (1999)

Jennifer Lopez, "If You Had My Love" (1999)

Ricky Martin, "Livin' La Vida Loca" ("Livin' the Crazy Life," 1999)

Santana feat. Rob Thomas, "Smooth" (1999)

Shakira, "Whenever, Wherever" (2001)

Pitbull, "Give Me Everything" (2011)

Ximena Sariñana, "Tú y Yo" ("You and I," 2011)

Wisin and Yandel feat. Jennifer Lopez, "Follow the Leader" (2012)

MAJOR AWARDS

American Music Awards (AMAs): The American Music Awards are awarded based on polls of the public. TV host Dick Clark created the awards in 1973. In 2011 Jennifer Lopez won the Favorite Latin Artist category. Other 2011 AMA nominees included Enrique Iglesias and Pitbull.

ASCAP Latin Music Awards: The American Society of Composers, Authors and Publishers (ASCAP) honors the top Latin songwriters and publishers at these awards. The ceremony's highest honor is the Founders Award. It goes to artists who have helped pioneer Latin music and have inspired their fellow Latin artists. In 2012 the Founders Award went to Marc Anthony.

The Billboard Latin Music Awards: The Billboard Latin Music Awards ceremony is broadcast annually on the Telemundo TV network. These awards honor the highest-charting Latin artists of the year. The ceremony includes a Lifetime Achievement Award as well as a Spirit of Hope Award that honors humanitarian achievements. In 2012 Latin music rising star Prince Royce won the Artist of the Year award.

The Grammy Awards: The Grammys are prestigious music awards given yearly since 1959 by the National Academy of Recording Arts and Sciences. In 2012 the Grammys included four awards in the Latin Music category. The Mexican rock band Mana won the award for Best Latin Pop, Rock or Urban Album with *Drama y Luz* (*Drama and Light*).

The Latin Grammys: One of the biggest events of the year for the Latin music scene is the Latin Grammys. This award ceremony is held annually by the Latin Academy of Recording Arts and Sciences. It celebrates the diversity of Latin music. The Latin Grammys were first held in 2000. Awards are given to the best artists in a wide variety of categories, including pop, rock, tropical, Mexican, Brazilian, traditional, and more. In 2011 *Calle 13* won the Latin Grammy for Album of the Year, *Entren Los Que Quieran* (*Those Who Want to Answer*), while Shakira won Best Female Pop Vocal Album for *Sale el Sol* (*Rising Sun*).

MTV Video Music Awards (VMAs): Latin stars often shine at the MTV network's annual Video Music Awards ceremony. These awards honor the best in music videos from a broad range of musical genres. In 2011 the Best Latino Artist VMA went to the reggaeton duo Wisin and Yandel.

SOURCE NOTES

10 R. J. Deluke, "Arturo O'Farrill: Upholding the Latin Tinge," *All About Jazz*, June 22, 2009, http://www.allaboutjazz.com/php/article.php?id=33194 (December 14, 2011).

11 Alan Lomax, *Mister Jelly Roll: The Fortunes of Jelly Roll Morton, New Orleans Creole and "Inventor of Jazz"* (Berkeley: University of California Press, 1973), 62.

24–25 Daniel Fischlin, ed., *Rebel Musics: Human Rights, Resistant Sounds, and the Politics of Music Making* (Montreal: Black Rose Books, 2003), 203

25 Ed Morales, *The Latin Beat: The Rhythms and Roots of Latin Music from Bossa Nova to Salsa and Beyond* (Cambridge, MA: Da Capo Press, 2003), 56.

27 "Faces of Salsa Quotes by Willie Colón," Willie Colon, February 28, 2009, http://williecolon.com/news/2009/02/28/faces-of-salsa-quotes (December 20, 2011).

39 Walter Martinez, "Selena Interview 2," *Latin Music Forever*, 1995, http://www.selenaforever.com/SelenaInterviews/Selena_Interview_2.html (April 14, 2012).

40 Betto Arcos, "Interview with Juan de Marcos González," PBS, January 1, 1998, http://www.pbs.org/buenavista/musicians/bios/demarcos_edited_int_eng.html (January 6, 2012).

44 Ricky Martin, quoted in Katherine Thompson, "Rick Martin Comes Out: 'I'm a Fortunate Homosexual Man,'" *Huffington Post*, May 29, 2010, http://www.huffingtonpost.com/2010/03/29/ricky-martin-comes-out-im_n_517625.html (April 4, 2012).

45 Henri Béhar, "Jennifer Lopez on Selena," Film Scouts, n.d., http://www.filmscouts.com/scripts/interview.cfm?File=jen-lop (December 30, 2011).

48 Larry Rohter, "A Master of Crossover Relives '70s Ballads," *New York Times*, June 18, 2010, http://www.nytimes.com/2010/06/19/arts/music/19anthony.html (January 3, 2012).

50 Mim Udovitch, "Q&A: Shakira," *Rolling Stone*, January 23, 2002, http://web.archive.org/web/20090207181309/http://www.rollingstone.com/artists/shakira/articles/story/5931811/qa_shakira (January 4, 2012).

SELECTED BIBLIOGRAPHY

Aparicio, Frances R., and Candida Jaquez, eds. *Musical Migrations: Transnationalism and Cultural Hybridity in Latin/o America.* Vol. 1. New York: Palgrave MacMillan, 2003.

Castro, Ruy. *Bossa Nova: The Story of the Brazilian Music That Seduced the World.* Translated by Lysa Salsbury. Chicago: A Cappella Books, 2000.

Catapano, Peter. "A Blending of Latin Sounds." *New York Times.* N.d. http://www.nytimes.com/library/music/102400salsa-essay.html (January 12, 2012).

Fernandez, Raul A. *From Afro-Cuban Rhythms to Latin Jazz.* Berkeley: University of California Press, 2006.

Guillermoprieto, Alma. *Samba.* New York: Vintage Books, 1991.

McGowan, Chris, and Ricardo Pessanha. *The Brazilian Sound: Samba, Bossa Nova, and the Popular Music of Brazil.* Philadelphia: Temple University Press, 2009.

Morales, Ed. *The Latin Beat: The Rhythms and Roots of Latin Music from Bossa Nova to Salsa and Beyond.* Cambridge, MA: Da Capo Press, 2003.

Roberts, John Storm. *The Latin Tinge: The Impact of Latin American Music on the United States.* New York: Oxford University Press, 1999.

Roy, Maya. *Cuban Music: From Son and Rumba to the Buena Vista Social Club and Timba Cubana.* Translated by Denise Asfar and Gabriel Asfar. Princeton, NJ: Markus Wiener Publishers, 2002.

Sublette, Ned. *Cuba and Its Music: From the First Drums to the Mambo.* Chicago: Chicago Review Press, 2004.

Thompson, Robert Farris. *Tango: The Art History of Love.* New York: Pantheon Books, 2005.

FURTHER READING, WEBSITES, AND FILMS

Accordion Dreams

http://www.pbs.org/accordiondreams/main/index.html
This PBS site is devoted to Tejano music. Check out a time-line, learn more about the accordion, and discover fun facts about Tejano music.

Alt.Latino

http://www.npr.org/blogs/altlatino
This blog from National Public Radio is devoted to all things Latino. Read about the latest in Latin music, check out rec-ommended songs and videos, and leave a comment if there's anything you want to discuss.

Cartlidge, Cherese. *Celia Cruz.* New York: Chelsea House, 2010.

Learn more about Celia Cruz, one of the legends of salsa music, from her beginnings in Cuba to her worldwide stardom later in life. The author gives a detailed biography of Cruz and her rise to fame.

Latin Beat

http://www.latinbeatmagazine.com
This site from *Latin Beat* magazine provides an in-depth look at what's going on in modern Latin music. Check out news, artist profiles, reviews, concert dates, and much more.

Latin Music USA. DVD. Directed by Pamela A. Aguilar and Daniel McCabe. Boston: PBS, 2009.

Actor Jimmy Smits hosts this four-part documentary about the history of Latin music. Hear a wide range of Latin songs from across the decades and see some of the faces that made Latin music an international success. Viewers can watch all four segments at http://video.pbs.org/program/latin-music-usa.

Latin Recording Academy

http://www.latingrammy.com/en/home
The home page of the Latin Grammys is loaded with information about the awards ceremony, award nominees and winners, and future events. Visitors can also check out recent performance videos.

Lindeen, Mary. *Cool Latin Music: Create & Appreciate What Makes Music Great!* Edina, MN: ABDO, 2008.

Read more about the history of Latin music, the instruments that Latin musicians use, and famous Latin artists. This book also helps readers write their own salsa song and learn to dance the samba!

Makosz, Rory. *Latino Arts and Their Influence on the United States: Songs, Dreams, and Dances.* Philadelphia: Mason Crest Publishers, 2006.

With this book, readers can explore the history and devel-opment of Latino art—including music—and learn about the ways in which Latino artists shaped American popular culture.

Murcia, Rebecca Thatcher. *Shakira.* Hockessin, DE: Mitchell Lane, 2008.

Shakira is one of Latin pop music's boldest stars. This short biography details Shakira's early life, her rise to fame, and her ability to stay at the top of the charts.

Nelson, Robin. *Selena Gomez: Pop Star and Actress.* Minneapo-lis: Lerner Publications, 2013.

Check out this book for more information about Selena Gomez, a Texas-born pop star of Mexican heritage. Readers can follow Gomez's path to fame and get the scoop on her relationship with music superstar Justin Bieber.

Thomas, Isabel. *Latin Dance.* Minneapolis: Lerner Publications, 2012.

This fun book captures all the excitement and glamour of Latin dance. Take a closer look at dances such as the stylish rumba, the lively cha-cha, and the passionate tango, as well as the salsa and the samba.

INDEX

ABOUT THE AUTHOR

Matt Doeden is a freelance author and editor. He has written hundreds of children's and young adult books covering areas such as sports, the military, cars and motorcycles, geography and, of course, music. He and his family live in Minnesota.

PHOTO ACKNOWLEDGMENTS

The images in this book are used with the permission of: © Kevork Djansezian/Getty Images, p. 1; © PM Images/Stone/Getty Images, pp. 2–3; © Leonard Adam/WireImage/Getty Images, p. 4; © Andy Sheppard/Redferns/Getty Images, p. 5 (left); © KMazur/WireImage/Getty Images, pp. 5 (right), 45; © Bruno Morandi/Robert Harding World Imagery/Getty Images, p. 6; © San Antonio Express-News/ZUMA Press, p. 7 (top left); © Waymoreawesomer/Dreamstime.com, p. 7 (top center); © Allexander/Dreamstime.com, p. 7 (top right); © Pablo Caridad/Dreamstime.com, p. 7 (middle left); © C Squared Studios/Photodisc/Getty Images, p. 7 (middle center); © iStockphoto.com/Lebazele, p. 7 (middle right); © Vlue/Dreamstime.com, p. 7 (bottom left); © Marka/SuperStock, p. 7 (bottom center); © Paul Piebinga/Photodisc/Getty Images, p. 7 (bottom right); Courtesy of Havana Collectibles, pp. 8, 9, 16; © CORBIS, p. 11; Courtesy Everett Collection, pp. 12, 14; © Bettmann/CORBIS, p. 13; © Hulton Archive/Getty Images, p. 15; © Hank Olen/NY Daily News Archive/Getty Images, p. 17 (left); © Metronome/Archive Photos/Getty Images, p. 17 (right); © Michael Ochs Archives/Getty Images, pp. 18 (top and bottom left), 20, 26 (right), 28 (bottom); © Gai Terrell/Redferns/Getty Images, p. 18 (bottom right); © iStockphoto.com/hudiemm, pp. 19, 31 (right), 41 (bottom), 55, 57, 59, 61, 63; © Tucker Ransom/Hulton Archive/Getty Images, p. 21; El Mercurio de Chile/Newscom, p. 22 (top); © ZUMA Wire Service/Alamy, p. 22 (bottom); AP Photo/Prensa Latina/Jose A. Figueroa, p. 23; REUTERS/Handout, p. 24; © Andrew Lepley/Redferns/Getty Images, p. 25; © Tom Copi/Michael Ochs Archives/Getty Images, p. 26 (left); AP Photo/Andres Leighton, pp. 27, 35; © Joe Conzo/Retna Ltd., p. 28 (top); © Jeffrey Thurnher/CORBIS, p. 29; © John Parra/Getty Images, p. 30 (left); © GAB Archive/Redferns/Getty Images, p. 30 (right); © Gary Null/NBC/NBCU Photo Bank via Getty Images, p. 31 (left); AP Photo/Bill Cooke, p. 32; © Sherry Rayn Barnett/Michael Ochs Archives/Getty Images, p. 33; © Travel Ink/Gallo Images/Getty Images, p. 34; © Angel Delgado/Clasos.com/LatinContent/Getty Images, p. 36 (left); © Ashley Maile/Retna/Photoshot, p. 36 (right); © RD/Kabik/Retna Digital/Retna Ltd., p. 37; © Arlene Richie/Media Sources/Time & Life Pictures/Getty Images, p. 39; © Jorge Silve/AFP/Getty Images, p. 40 (top and second from top); Crawford Brown/Rex USA, p. 40 (second from bottom); © Bernd Muller/Redferns/Getty Images, p. 40 (bottom); © Warner Bros./Courtesy Everett Collection, p. 41 (top); © SGranitz/WireImage/Getty Images, p. 42; © DMI/Time & Life Pictures/Getty Images, p. 43; © Jon Kopaloff/FilmMagic/Getty Images, p. 46 (left); © s_buckley/Shutterstock.com, p. 46 (right); © Ethan Miller/Getty Images, p. 47; © Kevin Winter/Getty Images, p. 48; © Clayton Call/Redferns/Getty Images, p. 49; © Stuart Franklin/Getty Images, p. 51; © Jeff Kravitz/FilmMagic/Getty Images, p. 52; © Kelly A. Swift/Retna Ltd., p. 53; © Noel Vasquez/Getty Images, p. 54.

Front cover: © iStockphoto.com/Jacom Stephens. Back cover: © iStockphoto.com/hudiemm.

Main body text set in Arta Std Book 12/14. Typeface provided by International Typeface Corp.